TYOLOGY: ESSENCE OF LIFE

by

TYRA J. HICKS

ISBN 978-1-7321298-0-1

Copyright © 2018 by Tyra J. Hicks

All rights reserved. No part of this publication may be reproduced, distributed, or transmitted in any form or by any means, including photocopying, recording, or other electronic or mechanical methods, without the prior written permission of the publisher, except in the case of brief quotations embodied in critical reviews and certain other noncommercial uses permitted by copyright law.

Printed in the United States of America.

Foreword

What is Tyology?

Tyology is the study of Tyra's mind. To understand life, a person must first understand themselves. I have encountered many things in my life that has provided me with the insight of life differently from others. As a life coach and counselor, I have different perceptions on how daily life hiccups can deter a person from their designed purpose. This book touches on a vast amount of everyday life struggles and stressors that we all either faced or will face in due time. I can only speak from my experiences and share my outcome from weathering the storm. I pray that my words provide you with a sense of awareness to your own life and the people in it.

Be encouraged!

Table of Contents

Ambition   5

Awareness 18

Bliss 36

Character 41

Discernment 60

Essence of Life 67

Faithfulness 95

Inquest   108

Insight   114

Life Lessons of Tyra   138

Modesty 200

Productivity 208

Progression 222

Pursuit of Guidance 232

Tranquility 250

Afterword 259

Ambition

Moves

Keep all your dreams and moves to yourself. Move in silence always.

Support Yourself

Support your own dreams. Never wait for someone to validate your dream. Be your own cheerleader and biggest fan.

Push Forward

Always push yourself forward. Never go backwards. We don't have eyes in the back of our heads for a reason.

Investment

Don't spend all your time investing into someone else's vision that you put your dreams on the back burner. No matter what always make time to make your vision a reality.

Mentality

Embrace your seven-figure mentality.

If you don't think highly of yourself,

who else will.

Self-investment

Invest in yourself, just like you have been investing in other people's dreams. As much time you spend at work, accommodating someone else's dreams; how about you spend triple that time on yourself. Create your own business. Never settle to just be an employee. Strive to be the boss.

<u>Build Up</u>

Work on yourself to build your self-worth. Ignite the power you have within you. Sound understanding of your own perceptions of yourself will increase self-love and your self-esteem.

Life Plan

Don't know what to do with our life?

Set S.M.A.R.T goals.

Implement a deadline for your goals.

Create your life plan and execute it!

Self

Advocate, Market and Promote yourself!

Determination

Determination comes from within

Determination drives ambition

Determination fuels hunger

Hunger fuels success

Scripting

Do you do the same thing day in and day out? Are you tired of dealing with the same type of people? Does it seem like you always experience the same outcome? Stop sticking to the script. Go outside the box and try something different to get a different result.

Focusing

Never lose focus on your target.

If you want it, go get it!

Awareness

Elevation

Recognize your elevation and release the dead weight. Holding on to dead weight will halt your elevation.

Self-Awareness

I respect and love myself enough to walk away from anything that no longer serves me, grows me, or makes me happy.

Pain

Pain is the best teacher. It awakes your senses and forces you to pay attention. The pain you have endured, will teach you about yourself.

Positive Self-Talk

Never put yourself down!

Never back down!

Never stop dreaming!

Be the best you, you can possibly be

Never give up!

Truth

Stop lying to yourself. Stop holding on to useless and unworthy people that drains your spirit to just have a warm body.

You can do bad by yourself.

Be true to yourself!

Inspiration

Learn something new

Continue to grow as a person

Discipline yourself to maintain positivity

Surround yourself with people who will push you to achieving greatness.

Stay inspired!

The elements of self:

acceptance, love, worth, esteem

understanding, awareness, confidence,

reflection, perseveration, respect

To manipulate or not

Many people have power over other's and can use it for good or bad. However, it takes a powerful person to relate to others than to dominate them.

Acceptance

We are all created in God's image. Accept people for who they are, instead of belittling them. Treat others how you expect to be treated.

Patience

Take the time to get to know yourself,

to redeem your strength and

refocus on your purpose.

Placement

Decipher who is real and fake in your life. Decipher their role in your Recognize your place in someone's life.

Weaknesses

Everyone has weaknesses. Every weakness can be implemented into a strength. Acknowledge what your weaknesses and strengths are. Face your weaknesses head on. Push through the difficulty until you prevail. Stay positive through the process and watch what your weaknesses manifest into strength.

Validation

Everyone likes to be complimented from to time to time. It becomes a problem, when you do things to just got a "job well done" compliment from someone. Acknowledge your own gifts and talents. Be confident in yourself. Don't look for validation in others. Validate yourself!

Positive outcomes

Look for the positive in all situations. You can turn a negative situation to a positive outcome. Recognize what you view as a negative is a positive. Everything happens for a reason. God removes things from your life for something better.

Attention

Not all attention is good attention. Be advised of the way you present yourself in public and private. Sometimes a person attracts and accept anything just to feel a part of something.

Favor

Do yourself a favor and identify, examine, and get to know yourself first and foremost. Self-worth and self-confidence is a major key.

Speak it!

Nobody can tell your story better than you. Always speak your truth and stand in it!

Bliss

Laughing

Laughter is good for the soul and your spirit; laugh often!

Laughter

Laughter diminishes the presence of depression.

Live

Go out and do something worthwhile.

Stop living up to someone else's standards. Establish your own.

Don't be afraid to LIVE!!

Happiness

Happiness is found within not through other people. Learn to love yourself first and believe in yourself before you can expect any kind of relationship to work. If you don't love yourself how do you expect someone else to love you. Know your worth and never settle for less. Remember you can do bad by yourself.

Character

Who are you?

Walk it, like you talk it!

(Be whom you proclaim to be)

Self-Love

Self-love is the best love!

No one can love you better than

you can love yourself.

Love thyself

Are you feeling like you cannot press forward? Love thyself! Are you feeling loss and thrown away? Love thyself! Feeling unloved? Love thyself!

Never give up on yourself; always love yourself and press forward thorough all storms. Remember light will always outshine darkness. Love thyself first and foremost. Love thyself, before you can love another!

Struggles

Every struggle you have encountered and overcame has impacted your life for the better and built your character.

Never Give Up

Never give up on yourself, or your goals.

Keep striving to become a

better version on you!

Authenticity

Dare to be different.

Why be a carbon copy of another;

when we were created to stand out.

Self-Worth

You are worthy of love and respect. Honor your body, mind and spirit. Recognize your value. Never settle for disrespect. Acknowledge your self-worth!

Love, Honor & Appreciate thyself

When people are so judgmental to the moves you make. Love yours!

When your happy and faced with hate from others. Love yours!

When you are radiating and glooming in success and people, start to assassinate your character. Love yours!

People will always be people, don't let the negativity of some sabotage the goodness of your spirit. Love yours!

Don't switch up!

Never change who you are for anybody. Your morals and values are part of your character. Your character defines who you are. Don't change yourself to impress someone else.

Courageous

It takes courage to reveal your insecurities. It takes courage to trust someone who have hurt you. It takes courage to love again after heartbreak. It takes courage to be yourself in a world full of doppelgangers. Be courageous.

Stand firm

Always stand your ground

Say what you mean and mean what you say. Stand firm and never falter!

Realization

People need to realize it's not always about them and their feelings. It is bigger than them and other people have feelings as well. Treat others like you want to be treated. It's always the small things that matters the most.

Believe

Your life has meaning. Your life has a purpose. Believe in yourself, because life is worth living. Cherish the life you have.

Bitterness

Don't let painful experiences change you to become hateful and bitter.

Do you want it, or do you deserve it?

Do you want it? Do you deserve it?

Forget what you want and

remember what you deserve!

Transparency

Be transparent.

Transparency shows your true self and openness of your heart.

Discernment

Fuel

People will never want you to do better than them. Let the negativity fuel your greatness.

Evolution of self

Change is inevitable and hard to adapt to at times. Change is the way of life and the evolution of self.

Embrace change.

Elevation

As you begin to elevate, life around you begin to shift. Your mind becomes clearer and your focus becomes keener. Elevation provides you with clarity and perspective.

Blessed

Realize that you are blessed beyond measure and everything that is attached you shall prosper!

Love

Love outweighs all negativity.

Love will always win;

no matter how much hate is present!

Process

Nobody has all the answers. Nobody has a perfect life. We are all a work in progress. We are all striving to survive and better provide for our families. Success doesn't happen overnight. Trust the process!

Essence of Life

Money

Money and materialistic items

does not bring happiness;

only debt and disappointments

Storms

Even though storms may brew.

Nobody can ever rain on your parade

because the sun is always shining on

you.

Divine Delay

People are always looking for a quick fix to the things that happens in their life. Everything you experience has a lesson in it. Take a step back and re-evaluate yourself and the situation at hand. You have all the answers to your problems, if you trust the process of timing. Just because you see somebody else receiving a blessing and you are wondering when yours is coming; trust the process!!!

Your time has not come yet but when it comes; you will be ready to receive it and soar like you are destined to do.

Fathers

Being a father is just not supplying your DNA. Being a father is becoming a man and being responsible for the life you helped create. My love and appreciation go out to the fathers who do the work effortlessly. There may be struggles along the way, but you never leave your children in despair or disappear out of their lives. Continue to instill in your children morals and values.

Standing in the gap

Not all men are absent fathers.

Many men step in and become

role models to other people's children.

Friendships

Every friendship has different dynamics. The dynamics are established by the chemistry the individuals have. Every friend has a purpose and a season in your life. Not every person you call a friend is a friend. Understand the difference between an acquaintance and a friend.

Respect

Respect is earned, not given.

Never let anyone disrespect you,

no matter who they are or their title.

Treat me like you want to be treated.

Motherhood

Being a mother is a journey. Mother hood is an adventure that never ends. Each level is full of different circumstances. Never let a man that is not your child's father physically discipline them. Never put a man before you child. Always put your children as your priority.

Life's pleasures

The simple pleasures in life is being able to have inner peace and stability.

Worthy

Nothing worth having will come easy and you will have to fight for the things you want in life. Nothing is handed to you in this world. Nothing is free. Everything has a cost.

Leaping

People always say that they want to try something new but are afraid to leap into faith. You have to go out there on that limb and jump. You must put action behind those ideas and dreams. Make it happen!

Incarcerated mind

We are products of our past,

but we do not have to have incarcerated

mindsets. Break free from the

standardized program.

Create your own destiny!

Appreciation

Develop an appreciation for the present because the past is gone and the future is not promised.

Shame

Never be ashamed for anything you have done. If you are ashamed of something you have done; then you shouldn't have done it. Love and live life with no regrets.

Priorities

A person makes time for the things that are important to them and the people they care about the most.

Get your priorities in order!

Moments

Life is about creating moments.

Create, capture, and enjoy life.

Be happy!

Ten toes down

Live life like its your last day on earth.

Live life without stress and disappointments. Live life carefree.

Live life like its golden.

Care switch

Calm your heart.

Learn how to turn the care off

from undeserving people and situations.

Turning the care off preserves your

emotional and mental stability.

Ownership

Take ownership of your own life

instead of trying to live

through other people.

Impacting others

Understand that you can't save them all. Realize that some don't want to be saved. Save the one's that are fighting to live. Make a difference one person at a time.

Damaged goods

We are all damaged goods but don't be afraid to give love another chance. Good men still exist. They just as damaged as us women.

The moment

Live in the moment,

tomorrow is

not promised.

Trust

Trust is hard to get

but

easy to lose.

Comfort

Be the comfort

in

your own storms.

<u>LGBTQ</u>

Love is love.

Spread love to everyone unwavering.

Accept people for who they are, not whom they choose to love.

Parenting

Having children does not, stop you from achieving your goals. Yes, it may cause a temporary delay but never put your dreams on the shelf. Always strive to become a better you. Be mindful that your children are always watching you.

Faithfulness

Pray

Why worry about it;

When you can pray about it.

Let go and let God fight your battles.

Loyalty

Loyalty is key to building relationships. A relationship is built on trust. Trust is established based on the loyalty shown. Being loyal is remaining true.

Losing Faith

Never lose your faith because, If God brought you to it, I have faith that he will bring you through it.

Blocked Blessings

Do not block your blessing by engaging in negativity. Your mouth can cause you to block your own blessings. Be mindful of the words you speak.

Confirmation

Claim it!

Speak it!

and it shall be.

Running on empty

Uplift your spirit

to

refuel your faith

Praise Break

Incorporate a praise break in your day

Always set aside time in your day to give honor and thank God.

Give yourself at least 6 seconds to praise God.

God's leadership

There's a big difference in your life, when you allow God to lead you instead of you trying to lead or go in your own direction.

Silhouette

Loyalty, faith, integrity, love and trust;

does not have a silhouette.

PUSH

Always push through,

no matter what the

circumstances

may be.

Get you together

Get yourself right first, before you expect God to come solve all your problems. God wants to see what you, can do yourself first. Stop waiting for others to try and fix you instead of fixing yourself.

Coach Ty's equation for God's Grace:

Dream + Attentiveness + Conquest

= God's Grace

Inquest

Seek Not

Seek not for what another has;

create your own empire!!

The Beacon

Seek God; as he is the beacon of light;

in the midst of the darkness.

Pray before you act out

I was in a dilemma as to be nasty or to remain unbothered. I asked God for direction. I received a message from God saying: Why would I tarnish my good spirit to inflict hurt on someone else. Yes, the hurt may only last temporarily but my spirit would be forever tarnished. Whom will hurt more? Myself! So, therefore I just prayed and let it go because at the end of the day I'm responsible for my own character. I stand for a lot and I refuse to let an irrelevant person dampen my spirit and hinder my blessings. We all make our own karma. What you put in is what you get back.

Guide

Lord, guide my footsteps into the

direction of the path,

I am destined to walk upon

Amen

Insight

Positivity

Positivity inspires others to be a better them.

Mental Stimulation

Mental stimulation is key to opening your mind to endless possibilities.

Inner Thoughts

Keep all your inner thoughts positive to reproduce positive performance to integrate positive customs.

Your conduct influences your positive obligations.

Dim light

Never dim your light to let someone else shine brighter than you; at your expense. Leave underserving people in the shadows.

Unbreakable

People will hate you for the things they see you with. Its only because they hate that you can go through things that were set up to break you. A miserable person cannot stand to see you came out on top and unblemished.

Distractions

Identify what's distracting you. You must eliminate all distractions. In order, to strengthen your focus.

True self

Get in touch with true self.

Do you know who you truly are?

Infusion

Infuse your life with action

to implement endless possibilities.

Integrity

Bad company

corrupts

good character.

Take Heed

Take heed to all situations.

Every message has a purpose.

Listen to the underline message.

Clouds

Every storm doesn't

brew up the

same clouds.

Disconnection

Recognize when it is time to cut people off and out of your life. The signs are always present.

Fearless

My advice to overcoming your fears:

Face them head on and never back down!

Hope

Never lose hope!

Endure all circumstances with love. This is the season of invisible hope and anything is possible.

Perceptions

A person's perception of you is just that. Their perception. It does not validate who you are. They just met your representative. Some people don't know the difference. Everyone is not worthy of knowing the real you.

Recognize the company you keep and present yourself accordingly. Everybody is not your friend.

Mindfulness

Be mindful of how people are around you during your shift in season.

Soul Snatchers

A person whom has no regard for life or have any ambitions will be the main naysayer on a decision you are making in your life. Remember one thing an empty wagon makes the most noise.

Hater

Sometimes it's the people whom are the closest to you that are the most envious.

Intuition

Always trust your intuition.

It will never steer you in the wrong direction.

The Drop

Sometimes we got to get knocked down,

to bring some things into prospective.

Disappointment

Disappointment only transpires when you establish expectations. If you don't expect anything, you won't get disappointed. Accept things for what they are.

Importance

Never lose focus

on what's important.

Life Lessons of Tyra

A Secure Woman

My definition of a secure woman is a woman who is secure in herself enough to empowers others. A secure woman forgives quickly but never forgets. A secure woman knows her worth and can recognize when it is time to leave. A secure woman exemplifies poise and grace.

Coach Ty's equation for simplicity of life:

Eat Good + Pray + Love + Grow + Live

= Simplicity of Life

Coach Ty's viewpoint:

Good Emotional Health =

Healthy Mental Health

Re-evaluate your circle

If they don't have goals and are not trying to achieve them keep them away from you. If they are still focused on the impressing others and gossiping; keep it to yourself. Associate yourself with others whom are securing the bag and building their own empire. Eliminate people who are cynical and criticize you on your decisions.

Advantage

Never take anything or

anyone for granted.

Show appreciation to all.

Discover your purpose

As I begin to ponder, it hits me. Not everybody is happy for you. You feel that you can share your good news with your friend, family, or spouse. Somewhere in the mix is, someone shouting "fake congratulations". Showing "fake love wearing a fake smile". My thing is if your counting on my downfall, well you will have to keep waiting. I may get knocked back a few steps, but I will never fall. I'm all about growth and being productive. My advice to you: whom are praying for my misfortunes use that time to ask God to help you, find your way and incorporate love in your heart. The way my heart is set up, I show love to everyone, no hate for anyone. If I don't rock with you, I don't associate with you. Be true to yourself; instead of trying to keep up with the next one. You will never know the exact struggle someone goes through, so stop trying to mirror your life like

somebody else. Focus on your life,

not anyone else's.

Acknowledge your truth

Everything that glitters ain't gold and every piece of gold isn't real. Just like every grass not greener on the other side. Think about why that grass is greener. It needed more nurturing, or it could be fake. Moral of the story: sometimes things are not what they seem.

Take time to get to the root of it instead of focusing on what you see on the surface. Sometimes it takes more than the naked eye to see the truth in things.

Jaded individuals

Envy, hate, or jealousy has not limits. People be aware that someone close to you could be the main one praying for your downfall. Showing fake empathy for your blessings and advancements. They be so caught up in your life that they don't realize that they can do the same thing you are doing. Work hard. Apply yourself. Do the work. Stay prayed up. Eliminate all snakes.

Prayer works

When things seem to be getting rough and you don't know which way to turn; turn to God. Just pray and keep praying. Storms don't last forever. You must be patient and remain humble. Pray in the intermission of the storm. He will see you though all your trials and tribulations.

Be the Blessing

Do something to make someone else's day better. It's not all about you all the time. Everybody is going through something. A kind word, a compliment, a laugh, a smile, or a hug could be something someone needs. Leave a good impression on someone today.

S.U.R.E.

S – Sacrificing

U – Understanding

R - Respectful

E – Empathic

Be for S.U.R.E.

in your relationships and life endeavors

Establishing a sound relationship

The thing about relationships that people fail to realize is that once they get the person they are pursuing; the consistency, persistence, and communication begins to lack and eventually die off. The other person will begin to lose interest. Once a person feels as if they don't matter, all interest fades and the deuces is thrown. It is important to know your worth and never settle for less than what you deserve.

There are plenty of sweet talkers, but ACTIONS will define a person's true intentions. Do not waste your time, energy, or put your life on hold for anybody. There is always somebody waiting to help you pick up the pieces when you at least expect it. We all have played the fool a time or two but focus on what you want and take care of yourself first. Everything else is obsolete.

Recognition of one's role

Leaves fly away and die. Branches break but roots last forever. What type of people do you have in your life?

Speculation

Everything ain't for everybody. Learn to keep something to yourself. The less people know the better. Let them speculate.

Forgiveness

To move past any hurt, you must forgive the one whom hurt you. To forgive them you must forgive yourself first. Forgiveness, is for you. It helps you to move past the hurt. By providing a sense of closure and strength to rebuild your life; without harboring over the issues and the person/people that has hurt you. Only start the forgiveness process when you can wholeheartedly commit to it. No need to forgive someone and keep talking about it or throwing it in their face every chance you get. Yet and still becoming bitter and showing animosity toward them. Forgive. Move on. Rebuild. Pray for strength and guidance but never forget.

The Grind

You can be the most educated person in the world but if you do not have a hustler's mentality, ambition, and common sense; you will never prevail.

Accountability

I'm at a point in my life that I refuse to give life to dead situations. If something just happened a minute ago, its dead to me. It comes with growth and realizing who and what you are. I don't need validation because I validate myself. I don't wait on anyone to do anything for me. I make it happen. I could care less about a promise someone has made because I can do it myself. I refuse to wait on anyone because time waits on no one. Nobody on this earth owe me anything or is obligated to do for me but myself. People need to learn how to take responsibility for themselves and their actions. Life don't owe you nothing and you made these decisions so deal with them. Be the best at the what you do. Anything that does not serve you is pointless. Stop being bitter. Be responsible for your actions.

Chess Move

Chess is played and won only by strategic planning and implementing of your moves. My view on my life is that it is a championship game of chess and my opponent is myself. For things to go as the are destined to be within my life, I must strategically plan and implement the right moves to get closer to the throne. My direction in life is all about making the right decisions and walking the right path to live a fulfilling life that I am destined to live comfortably.

Turning over a new leaf

Do not give life to irrelevant people. Do not be anyone's savior. I will not help others; who is not willing or putting in the effort of helping themselves. I will not entertain anyone's foolishness. If you didn't starve with me, you won't eat with me. There's no need for you try and weasel your way into my life. My train has limited seating and I'm the only one riding to my destination. I love me, and I refuse to let delayed people drain my spirit.

Standing your ground

Plant your feet, and stand your ground: My dad's advice to me: no matter what comes at you, always stand your ground. No matter what people say or do. Always stand your ground, no matter what. You are strong and can handle anything someone or something throws at you. Never give up because that's for the weak. Never show a person your weaknesses because they can use it against you. Always stand strong!

Coach Ty's 6 P's of Empowerment:

Pray, Persistence, Patience,

Plan, Prioritize, Perseverance

Disloyalty

Betrayal never comes from strangers, it is usually from your family or those closest to you.

Be cautious.

<u>Ever feel like you can't win for losing?</u>

To find a solution to your situation, you must first acknowledge that situation. Secondly, OWN your part in participating in the dysfunction to resolve the issue.

GRIT

Grit is a major component to success. Winning comes from enduring perseverance. Success coms from persistence and consistency with continually working toward your goal. Be aware of what you truly want and go get it.

Addiction

Relationships are a drug. It causes an addiction to another person. Some people get so, tied up and entangled with their mate; they lose sight of reality. You are an individual and never forget that. Never put more into a person than they are putting into you. Relationships are a team effort; not a competition to win over someone or one up them.

Finding your diamond

I have heard people say, I found my diamond, or I got a diamond in the ruff. My take on this saying is that; to understand what type of person you have (diamond), you must first recognize their value. Diamonds are expensive and beautifully shines as a polished finished product. Diamonds are created by pressure. However, to collect a diamond, the journey is life changing. Hard labor, blood, sweat, and tears goes into finding and sculpting these polished diamonds. With that being said, to reap the benefits of enjoying the beauty of that shiny, polished diamond; a person has to accept that uncut version (diamond in the ruff). With hard work, consistency, love, and nurturing your diamond in the ruff will become a well sculpted polished diamond on display.

The moral of the statement is to appreciate a person at their worse; if you expect to see them at their best. See the value in the individual. Some people need a little guidance and support to unleash their polished finishing. Empower, encourage and appreciate what you have.

Wisdom

Respect and listen to your elders. There's wisdom in the lesson they are trying to teach you.

Love or Lust

There is a difference between love and lust. Lust is overcoming with instant gratification of something you want. It fades. Love is when you see value in something and take care of it. It will last. Know the difference it can easily be misconstrued.

Trophy Wife

My perception of a trophy wife: a trophy wife is a woman whom has enchanting beauty but has nothing else to offer. In time, beauty fades. Beauty is in the eye of the beholder. What may be beautiful to you, may not attract another person. Beauty is not only physical but on a deeper spiritual, mental and emotional level. Why give someone the title of wife, when they are only an accessory instead of your equal. Trophies are made to be showcased and shelved for show that you have mastered something. Ladies, please have more respect for yourself and know your worth. Mentally stimulate your mate instead of making everything so accessible to him. Ask yourself: if you can be bought, does that mean you depreciate in value like materialistic objects?

Your husband will always have in his mind, if he can buy you, someone else can as well. Don't put a price tag on yourself.

Recognizing blockages

I had a dream that I was pulling up to a traffic light. My planned route was to turn right and continue my path home. It took my light a little longer than normal to turn green. I waited patiently. When my light turned green, as I was beginning to move; I had to make an abrupt stop. A work van began to back out the yard, directly at the light. I had a line of cars behind me so, I couldn't immediately go around. As the line of cars got shorter and shorter over a matter of minutes. The van had blocked my lane which was directed to either go straight or turn right at the light. The only open lane was the left turning lane. As I became, the final car still in position in that blocked lane; I backed up and veered to the left lane. However, considering the circumstances, I still made my right turn and continued the route home. The moral of the dream is that you can be on the path to achieve your goals and a block may appear out of nowhere. Don't let the block stop you. Find a detour or take an alternate route to get to your destination. I realized that sometimes you have to take a few steps backwards, take a few turns to get back on track but you will still get to your destination all the same. Just because you see other people arriving to their destination quicker than you, doesn't mean, you won't make it to yours. Don't get discouraged from another person's arrival of success. Timing is everything.

It's just not your time to arrive yet. God will confirm when your time is and if it is from God, nothing anyone can do will stop it.

Tighten Up

The pity party you have been throwing is over. Suck it up and move on. The party has been crashed. We all have trials and tribulations. You cannot continue to wallow in the same dysfunction and expect others to feel sorry for you. Get yourself together. Pray about, adjust your crown and move on back to business. Never give negative situations a lot of attention and energy. It will darken your spirit.

A man with a dream

A man with dreams and aspirations needs a woman with a vision. A woman will push, pray, and motivate her man to be great. She will never give up on you or let you give up on yourself. A woman will challenge you to depths you have never knew existed. Now if she does not; she is not the one for you. A woman whom is for you will have faith in you and your vision and will keep you focused on your goal. All the while she will be establishing her own vision.

Build together and motivate one another.

My philosophy on life

Life is hard. Life is full of twists, curves, blockages, hurdles, speed bumps that will cause you to experience a heap of unwanted emotions. Being able to handle your emotions will fuel you to question what your life's purpose. You will begin to question who am I? What am I supposed to be doing with my life? Why am I not at the level I desire to be? To become the person, you have visualized yourself to be; you must become that person. Speak that life on yourself. Claim that career. Set goals and achieve them. Never stop educating yourself on the betterment of self. Life is all what you make it.

Building up immature men

In a relationship, as a woman our job is to speak life into our man. To make him aware of his capabilities. However, in many cases from my own experience, you can build up the man and show him a whole different way of life and still get your heart broken. Immature men will accept the assistance to grow and reap all the benefits; until he has reached his level of success, then he does not need or want his woman's help anymore. The man will then begin to distance himself through lack of quality time and/or no communication until the woman gets tired of waiting and the relationship hits a dead end. No notice given, nor explanation will ever be provided. Identify the signs early to lessen the hurt.

The wolf in sheep's clothing

The I need help man: In the midst of the seasons changing from fall to winter; a vast number of male suitors will be reaching out to the available vulnerable women. They will say all the right things, treat you right, and show that they are so in love with you in a short period of time. Be cautious for those head over the heels individuals within a couple weeks to a months' time. That individual is not looking for a real relationship nor truly love you. He loves the need of you. He need a place to stay. He need to make sure that he does everything right so, he does not have to be homeless during the winter. Once it gets close to spring, see how fast you start to have arguments, fights, and him staying out late at night. Then you look up one day, the relationship is over! Just recognize the signs of a wolf in sheep's clothing because they prey on the weak.

Infidelity

We all have a wandering eye from time to time. It's called being human. Nothing is wrong with admiring the opposite sex from afar. The issue is when you, want to cross the line from a simple glance to being all up in someone's DMs. Why cheat, when you can leave. Nothing is more hurtful to a person, than being lied to and cheated on by the person that they loved wholeheartedly. Before you decide to cheat; think about your reasonings for it. What is causing you to lust after that person? Weigh your options? Talk to your mate about your predispositions before breaking their heart. Once the heart is broken, it takes time, forgiveness, patience, and effort to even get a margin of what the relationship was before the infraction.

Maturity

Age does not define maturity. Maturity is developed through growth and awareness. Most mature people have experienced some trials and tribulations that have caused them to grow up faster than others. Maturity defines your true character.

Single Mothers Anecdote

Single mothers are the most talked about group of individuals by all. We are frowned upon because we had children out of wedlock. We are considered damaged goods. We are looked at as being promiscuous if we have more than one child. People judge you before even knowing what your story is. We must do three times the work to ensure that our children have the bare necessities. We make a way out of no way, every birthday, holiday, and back to school. We never get a break. Our children may see us struggle but they will never go without the things they need. Sometimes you got to rob Peter to pay Paul, but you make it happen. Our children understand the value of dollar. We teach our children how to be humble and appreciate the small things. We sacrifice and compromise a lot to make sure our children are provided and cared for. We all had that white picket fence fairytale concept for our family but that was not the hand we were dealt. Single mothers are the most courageous and strongest women in this world. Salute ladies!

Modesty

Lift Up

Never talk down on another person.

Instead lift one another up but never underestimate anybody's potential.

Everybody has a due season.

Humble yourself

Humility will become your best teacher.

Your boasting will cause a chain reaction to force you to humble yourself.

Steady Pace

Stay consistent, put in the work,

don't lose focus and remain humble.

Empathy

Be empathic to others and their situation.

It can happen to you.

Self-Realization

When you are beating yourself up and think that you are not doing as good as you thought. Remember these things: You are blessed beyond measure. Be humble and thankful for what you have. There are people whom are doing way worse than you.

Reactions

Somethings occur to see how you will react. Somethings are set in place to break you. Somethings are there to destroy your spirit. If you stay prayed up, treat people right and remain humble; life will be so simple and less chaotic. Never let anything break you instead break away from all the negativity. Accept positive vibes only.

Boasting

Just because you have risen above your circumstances; does not mean for you to go around bragging and gloating about it. You should always remain humble. As quick as you rose up; it's even quicker to fall down.

Productivity

Consistency

Without consistency, you will never finish anything effectively and efficiently.

Work Ethic

Perseverance and hard work will pay off in the end. Remember slow and steady always win the race.

Quality

Be an asset

not

a liability

Transformation

Be the change

instead of

just making a change.

Stress Management

Stress less

Pray more

and

Hustle harder

86,400

When God chooses to wake you up; you are given 24 hours to begin again. You can't use time from yesterday nor borrow time from tomorrow. You must do what you can in the present. We all have 86,400 seconds a day. How are you using your time efficiently? Don't put off today in hopes to complete it tomorrow. Tomorrow is not promised to anyone. Live for today. Live for the moment. Live for you. Live carefree. Stop worrying about what other people have or don't have. Focus on you and yours. Stop letting negative talk from other people hinder you from making a difference in your life. Change is expected. Growth is progress.

Live with no regrets.

You have been given 86,400 seconds.

Make it count.

Productivity

Work at a steady, consistent pace

versus

sporadically to yield positive results.

Grinding

Grind hard to

elevate your mind and spirit

but remain focused on refining

your craft

Action

Get up, make some moves, do something with your life. Can't keep complaining about the changes you want to make but do nothing about it.

End procrastinations today.

Lead or Follow

Be a leader not a follower.

Leaders think and find solutions.

Followers just complain about their

problems and never want to

be part of the solution.

Coach Ty's Mogul status equation:

Persistence + consistency + ambition + drive X grinding = Mogul

Visions

Write your vision into existence. If you don't write it down, it will remain a just a thought. Writing it out makes it real and a concrete action plan.

Progression

Comfortability:

Comfortability = no desire, lack of elevation. Settling!!! People who settle become STILL individuals. STILL individuals are complacent with their lives. STILL broke, STILL complaining, STILL dramafied. If you want to achieve and be successful in life, NEVER GET COMFORTABLE! Always make something happen whether minor or major. It's progress! As you elevate so, will your re-evaluation of yourself, career, and social circle. Don't be alarmed that the people you thought was your friend, turn out not be a part of your elevation. Not everyone is supposed to ride your coat tail on your come up.

Outgrowth

Outgrowing people is a part of growth. Everyone is not part of your come up. You must leave people behind. Everyone serves a purpose in your life. Pay attention to the ones whom always show up when its beneficial to them or when life is going good for you but when you're struggling…they nowhere to be found.

Stagnation

Don't get complacent in one position.

You can't be stagnant and expecting

to be successful.

Failure

My philosophy for failure: a failure is a learned experience. You learn how to not make the same mistakes that you did before. It challenges your mind to create new solutions to a problem to yield success.

Cycles

A repeated situation is set to teach you a lesson that you missed the first time around.

Grow

Growth is a form of maturity.

Don't be afraid to grow

and leave your comfort zone.

Shifting

Embrace the shift.

Switch the game up.

Always change how your move.

Never become predictable.

Coach Ty's success equation:

ambition + perseverance X consistency - doubt

= success to achieving your goals!

Pursuit of Guidance

No Rushing

Rushing causes you to miss out on important key details. Slow down. Life is not a race to the finish line.

Don't rush anything.

Remain patient.

The Flow

Create your own flow. Be the flow.

Everything in life is temporary.

Affirmations

I am fearless

I am strong

I am beautiful

I will not give up on myself

I can overcome all obstacles

I believe in myself

I value my life

I love my self

My life has meaning

Be A Parent

Be in your children lives.

Show them unconditional love and affection at home. You don't want your kids to be the ones out in the streets.

The streets don't love nobody!

Face it

Choose to face everything and rise

from it; instead of

running from everything.

Separation before elevation

Recognize the things that God separates you from. They are designed steps for you to elevate to the next level of your growth.

Keys

Old keys will never open new doors. The locks have been changed and I hold the master key. I'm only unlocking the door for people of worth. Everyone is not worthy of your time and energy. Some people are better left standing in the yard and never crossing the threshold because they are soul snatchers. People will lie, and steal their way back into your life only to poison the new life you have established. So, you can be miserable like them. Be wise and watch the company you keep and realize that every I am happy for you, Isn't!

Competition

Never be in competition with anyone.

Trust the process that God is putting

your through. You will reach your

destination at your designated time.

Company you keep

Surround yourself with likeminded individuals. Assets attract other assets not liabilities. If your circle are all bosses, you will be the next. If your circle are millionaires, you will be the next one. The company you keep will impact either your success or your demise.

Trials

Struggles are designed to knock you down but lean instead of falling backwards. Always fall frontward.

Preparation

Always stay prepared for any outcome

Expect the unexpected and

you'll never have

to get ready

Hear once but listen twice

Some people have your best interest at heart, but it's up to you to take heed to the information. I'm only going to tell you something one time and what you do with the information is entirely up to you. Life is too short to be wasting time on judgmental people. Pay attention to who you surround yourself with.

Dreamers

Nothing comes to a dreamer, who doesn't make the dream a reality. Decipher your dream into words. Write your vision. Once you write it down, it becomes concrete. It becomes a thing. That thing becomes your goal. Do the work to make it happen.

Word of Choice: Tenacity

Re-evaluate your success squad! Some people whom are "friends" will be downgraded to acquaintances. I'm all about positivity and growth. You do not or will not need a sour puss around you. Do not join in any foolishness. The more they pray on your down fall, the harder you go. Realize that you were made from greatness and you will not falter. Your mission in life is growth and prosperity.

Obstacles

Everyone experiences blockages. It's just about finding detours to go around it or creating a way to demolish it. Either go around, go through it, or sit and wait until it decides to move.

The choice is yours.

Tranquility

Inner Peace

Do not let the actions of others hinder your inner peace.

Muted

Silence your mind to listen

to the directions of your life.

Coach Ty's equation for inner peace:

Pray + Forgiveness + Love one another

= inner peace

Silence

Your silence speaks volumes. You don't have to respond to everything. Your silence will speak for you better than any words you could fathom to speak.

Active Listening

Stop looking for a reason to respond instead just stop talking and listen.

Coach Ty's tranquility equation:

Get quiet + calm state + inner peace

= a state of tranquility

Clutter

Our minds run all day long, which causes it to become cluttered. In order for the mind to declutter, you have to get into a calm state. Take some time today and get quiet to clear you mind. You can't see where your supposed to be going if you don't clear a path.

Peace and Quiet

Learn to let your mind and body rest. The mind and body must reboot to remain sharp. Be still today and quiet your mind. Let God work it out!

Afterword

I hope that my experiences from my storms and growth has provided you with the insight to incorporate a change in some things in your life. Dealing with broken promises, mistreatment from friends and family has made me wiser. You can weather any storm that may brew, if you stay prayed up and be optimistic. Pay attention to all signs that

God sends you; to guide your footsteps

in walking in your purpose.

Be Blessed ♥

NOTES:

www.ingramcontent.com/pod-product-compliance
Lightning Source LLC
Chambersburg PA
CBHW061635040426
42446CB00010B/1425